LAST YEARS OF THE
LONDON
TITAN

LAST YEARS OF THE
LONDON
TITAN

PEN & SWORD
TRANSPORT
AN IMPRINT OF PEN & SWORD BOOKS LTD
YORKSHIRE · PHILADELPHIA

MATTHEW WHARMBY

CONTENTS

Front cover: Stagecoach East London **T 163** (CUL 163V) at Romford, 21 April 1999.

Back cover, top: Blue Triangle **T 349** (KYV 349X) at Croydon, 29 August 1999.

Back cover, middle: London Central **T 1111** (B111 WUV) at Crystal Palace, 11 August 1999.

Back cover, bottom: Stagecoach Selkent **T 885** (A885 SUL) at Bromley South, 22 April 1999.

Title page: London Central **T 787** (OHV 787Y) at Bexleyheath, 20 March 1999.

ISBN 978 1 52674 971 0

Published in 2019 by Pen & Sword Transport
an imprint of Pen & Sword Books Ltd, 47 Church Street,
Barnsley, South Yorkshire, S70 2AS

Typeset by Matthew Wharmby
Printed and bound in India by Replika Press Pvt. Ltd

Pen & Sword Books Ltd incorporates the imprints of Pen & Sword Archaeology, Atlas, Aviation, Battleground, Discovery, Family History, History, Maritime, Military, Naval, Politics, Railways, Select, Transport, True Crime, and Fiction, Frontline Books, Leo Cooper, Praetorian Press, Seaforth Publishing and Wharncliffe.

For a complete list of Pen & Sword titles please contact
PEN & SWORD BOOKS LIMITED
47 Church Street, Barnsley, South Yorkshire, S70 2AS,
England
E-mail: enquiries@pen-and-sword.co.uk
Website: www.pen-and-sword.co.uk

INTRODUCTION

This book begins as the Titan's career in London was winding down. The second-hand buses had completed their short tours of duty back in London and all that remained by the beginning of 1998 were the stalwart fleets that Stagecoach East London, Stagecoach Selkent and London Central had inherited from London Buses Ltd after privatisation. Joining them were the small complements still available to Blue Triangle and Sovereign, and from time to time emergency deployments would still figure, like First Capital's hired Ts on the 1 and the 185's first two weeks with the latterly infamous London Easylink. Milling around the edges at weekends, as the London Underground system creaked under the sheer weight of passenger numbers without the benefit of regular maintenance on the old pattern, were Titans on rail replacement services before what later became Transport for London demanded, as with its normal bus routes, that low-floor buses prevail.

There's no superfluous glamour in this book. The roughly five hundred Titans still in service, in their mid-to-late teens by the period covered, had been compelled to serve rather longer than expected due to the upheaval surrounding tendering and privatisation, and were mostly in the state you'd expect from spending twenty hours a day pounding London's streets, but by the turn of the century their replacement by low-floor buses was well in hand. Stagecoach's two halves had retired their Ts by the autumn of 2001, and London Central held out for another eighteen months.

Let this book form a salute to one of London's finest modern bus types, and long may the examples available to us now in preservation continue.

Matthew Wharmby
Walton-on-Thames
August 2018

Selkent District of the old London Transport came late to the Titan, not being scheduled for the type until the tail end of 1982, but most deliveries of the 1983 order (T 676-885) and 1984 order (T 886-1125) went there, entering service at Plumstead, Bexleyheath, Catford, New Cross and Bromley. Once DMS replacement was completed, attention was turned to ejecting RMs from south-east London's crew routes. **T 770** (OHV 770Y) was new to Bexleyheath in May 1983 but when that garage closed on 16 August 1986 passed to Sidcup, and thence to Catford on 16 January 1988 when Sidcup closed. It then spent April 1991 to April 1998 at Bromley before returning to Catford, on whose 185 it is seen at Victoria on 9 April 1999. Its last hurrah was at North Street between April and August 2001.

LONDON CENTRAL

No film was better than Ilford for classic black and white reproduction, even if New Cross's **T 1011** (A611 THV) was less pristine before the viewfinder than in London Transport days. At the start of the period covered by this book, London Central could muster 157 Titans for service, twenty-five of them being based at New Cross for the 1 and 172. T 1011 had been new to Plumstead but transferred to New Cross on 3 August 1985 and remained here ever since. On 3 June 1998 it is seen at the cramped and not particularly salubrious stand the 1 was compelled to occupy round the back of New Oxford Street.

New Cross's Ts also operated the 36 on Sundays when its RMs and RMLs took that day of the week off. With a Remembrance Day poppy wedged into its radiator grille, **T 1063** (A63 THX) heads round the back of Peckham on 24 May 1998. It spent the vast majority of its career at New Cross, only breaking that with six months at Bexleyheath at the end of 1993 and a final transfer there in February 2000, after which it was withdrawn.

T 1087 (B87 WUV) out of New Cross still has its original white-on-black London Transport numberplate with the unique and hard-to-replicate typescript when seen at new Oxford Street on 22 May 1998 (that on T 1011 opposite was a re-do with different transfers). This bus was to remain a New Cross bus all its life, spanning September 1984 to May 2001.

By mid-1998 Camberwell could put 45 Titans into the field, having suffered some losses with the conversion of the 35 and 40 to NV operation but still operating the largest number of Ts within London Central. Very much a stopgap operation was the use of Camberwell Ts on the 196; although that combination was what this route had been converted to OPO with in 1982, it had been run in the decade and a half since then with Norwood Ms and then Ls, followed by Cityrama's rickety Fleetlines, London & Country ANs and then, more permanently with VCs from Stockwell. However, what became London General was suffering staff problems and had to call on its recently-acquired new sibling for help, hence this shot of **T 946** (A946 SYE) at Norwood Junction on 10 April 1998. This bus had been at Camberwell since new, but would pass to Bexleyheath twelve months after this picture was taken and finish its career there.

For a long time the longest route in London, the 12 had been pared back successively during the 1980s to settle on a Notting Hill Gate-Dulwich core, operated in two overlapping sections. On the afternoon of 24 May 1998 in Peckham we see Camberwell's **T 970** (A970 SYE). Perhaps because they continued the obsolete and uninspiring tapegrey livery inherited from London Buses, London Central's Titans always looked less well kept than their Stagecoach neighbours, which cemented their new identity with rapid repaints into a new livery again. The mismatched bumpers and empty PAY DRIVER panel don't help.

A decade after the infamous Bexleybus operation had turned this area of south-east London on its head, Bexleyheath garage itself had survived and gone on to become, once again, a major Titan user, which would continue under London Central stewardship. **T 1051** (A651 THV), seen at Woolwich on 16 December 1998, would go on to be one of the last four Ts at Bexleyheath, finally retiring in March 2002 .

The 3 had been converted to OPO on 4 January 1993 using 24 new Optare Spectras, but they were frequently backed up by Camberwell's existing Titans, and latterly in some strength. In June 1998 **T 982** (A982 SYE) is seen at the 3's Oxford Circus stand.

Long before it was decided to split the 63 into two and curtail the town section at Honor Oak, Peckham's **T 968** (A968 SYE) has arrived at the Crystal Palace stand on 17 May 1998. This is another one with a mismatched pair of bumpers, one carrying a hole but no foglight and on without anything at all. This was a more recent entrant to the garage, having transferred from Camberwell in November 1990 and lasting until March 2000, when the 63 received AVLs.

On 16 December 1998 **T 713** (OHV 713Y) reposes at Woolwich on the 51, operated out of Bexleyheath since 5 September 1992. It had been new to this garage but moved away even before the initial closure, serving at Plumstead and then Peckham before coming back in November 1990 to spend the rest of its career here. The 51 was officially NV-operated at this point, but Ts could still be counted on to lend help when needed.

Minibuses had swept away the old 70 in November 1998, but the resulting P11 was too much for the new StarRiders to handle, so the route was double-decked, first with existing Peckham Titans and then with nine new Alexander-bodied Volvo Olympians coded AV. On 25 July 1998 **T 1021** (A621 THV), with fleetnumber transfers repurposed from a numberplate and still carrying the old London Buses-derived unit logos, pauses at Rotherhithe. New to Plumstead, this bus would spend sixteen years at Peckham, coming off in May 2001.

The 12 had been OPO on Sundays and Bank Holidays since 1988, being the last route to go over, and 31 August 1998 was a Bank Holiday, prompting the appearance of Peckham Titans like **T 1078** (A78 THX), seen in Whitehall. This bus ran the gamut of south-east London sheds, but its longest spell was at Peckham.

This author was thrilled to see Titans finally make it to the 37 when, in order to alleviate staff shortages then plaguing London General, New Cross was given an allocation. It could have happened, were it not for New Cross's original small allocation having ben withdrawn upon the route's OPO conversion on 21 June 1986. On 21 May 1999 **T 1062** (A62 THX) is seen at Clapham Junction. This bus would spend its life at New Cross, with two short spells at Bexleyheath, the final one at the very end.

The confluence of Harrow Road and Elgin Avenue was where the 36 would have turned right anyway, but on Carnival days it was the extravaganza's northern pedestrian entrance and thus particularly busy. **T 937** (A937 SYE), only at New Cross since July 1998 but familiar with the garage from having served there briefly in 1993, is seen on 30 August.

On its way out of the maelstrom on 30 August 1998, **T 1085** (B85 WUV) enters the Harrow Road. This was another late entrant to New Cross, having been displaced from Camberwell by a new NV.

When espied at Woolwich, General Gordon Place on the morning of 16 December 1998, Bexleyheath's **T 701** (OHV 701Y) was devoid of fleetnames. Its last decade was spent at Bexleyheath and it was withdrawn at the end of 1999, even before the big replacement wave of PVLs.

The 89 was Bexleyheath's bread and butter, returning there after the fall of Bexleybus but retaining a New Cross proportion for another decade. Titans were the staple until 2000, and on 23 March 1999 New Cross's **T 1062** (A62 THX) is seen at Bexleyheath Broadway, where construction was about to begin on a building which would obscure this otherwise ideal photo spot. T 1062 remained able to work the 89 after the loss of the New Cross share, transferring to Bexleyheath where it would spend the last two years of its career.

Although the passage of time had cost **T 1086** (B86 WUV) its opening front upper-deck windows, its PAY DRIVER plate and its foglights, it still managed to hold onto its original numberplate and larger-sized Leyland badge when seen at Hyde Park Corner on 25 April 1999. The career of this late Titan had been more varied than most of its number block, encompassing Plumstead, Bexleyheath, Sidcup, New Cross and finally Peckham, from where it was withdrawn in April 2002.

Equipped with a dot-matrix blind so as to be able to cover the Night Bus network in its entirety, Camberwell's **T 1005** (A605 THV) is seen in Oxford Street on 25 April 1999.

The circuitous 45 was split in 1990, its western shank becoming first 45A and then 345. LDPs were in charge after 1997, but the single-doored Dart SLFs struggled so badly with this tremendously busy route that Titans like lifelong New Cross **T 1059** (A59 THX), seen at Clapham Common on 21 June 1999, had to help out.

On 6 March 1999 at Clapham Junction, **T 1085** (B85 WUV) holds down the 37's temporary New Cross allocation, which was withdrawn on 4 May.

This may be a book about Titans, but they don't have it all their own way; on 21 May 1999 Camberwell's **T 716** (OHV 716Y) has taken it upon itself to break down right in the middle of St John's Road, impeding the progress of the large number of buses needing to use this important thoroughfare to Clapham Junction. Accordingly, Volvo Olympian **NV 73** (R273 LGH) has caught up to it and is attempting to get past; disregard the blinds, it really is another 35! NVs had indeed been the permanent allocation since 1997, but not from that batch; NV 73 had been delivered for the 21. T 716 was sold in February 2000.

A creation of Bexleybus, the 492 had settled down as a 'London Transport' bus route and indeed, upon its takeover by London Central on 23 January 1999, regained double-deckers since its days with LSs, first from Bexleybus and then, by necessity, from Boro'Line Maidstone. **T 752** (OHV 752Y), based locally since January 1991, is seen at Bexleyheath on 20 March 1999.

The 469 was also a child of Bexleybus, seeing out most of the 1990s with Bexleybus T operation, but upon its retention by London Central on 23 January 1999, was converted to DRL operation and rerouted via backstreets. Prior to that change, **T 766** (OHV 766Y) is in Woolwich on 16 December 1998. At the start of this bus's life, it had undertaken an unusual deployment, serving at Westbourne Park as a crew bus alongside Metrobuses on the 18.

Very few Titans were re-registered with former RM marks, by contrast with Metrobuses and VCs, but in January 1994 **T 735** gained WLT 735. On 20 March 1999 it is seen on the 229 at Bexleyheath.

When the massive Bluewater out-of-town shopping mall opened in 1999, two London bus routes were extended from Dartford to serve it. One was the 492, still operated with Bexleybus Titans like re-registered **T 735** (WLT 735, ex-OHV 735Y). It is seen on 1 May 1999 in the bus station carved out of the chalk pit in which Bluewater finds itself.

Finally for 23 January 1999, the 422 proved a major win for Bexleyheath. It had started as an LS route when Bexleybus bowed but was given to Boro'Line within a year, later falling foul of Boro'Line's own problems and passing to Kentish Bus. Now it was a major Bexleyheath Titan route, and indeed on 29 May 1999 was doubled in length through its extension from Woolwich to North Greenwich, a new station on the Jubilee Line Extension. On 20 March at Bexleyheath we see **T 889** (A889 SYE), fresh off a loan to Capital Citybus for the 1, which it worked previously when based at New Cross.

During the summer of 1999, the Bank branch of the Northern line was subjected to extensive works and thus replacement buses were put on. One of the operations was appended to the 133 as an extension to Euston, and one of its operators was London Central. On 21 July 1999 New Cross's **T 1064** (A64 THX) is seen at Moorgate, sporting the yellow band added over the top of LBL's grey skirt a few years after London Central got itself established. T 1064 had served only at New Cross since delivery in September 1984, but at the end of 1999 woudl transfer to Bexleyheath.

T 929 (A929 SYE) was best known for its dot-matrix blind box, but by 1999 it had been replaced with a conventional setup and on 25 May the bus is seen at Brixton on the 45. It had spent its first year and a quarter at Walworth, but since 3 August 1985 had served at Camberwell and would finish its career there.

There's work going on at Lewisham bus station on 6 August 1999 as the Docklands Light Railway tracks are laid to their new southern terminus, but it's not enough to impede photography of Bexleyheath's **T 1051** (A651 THV) laying over after another journey on the 89. Bexleyheath would be this bus's longest posting, but right before withdrawal in April 2002 (as one of the garage's last surviving four), it was sent to Camberwell and then New Cross to help out where needed.

Carrying the yellow band added to the basic tapegrey livery inherited from LBL, **T 871** (A871 SUL) heads down Oxford Street on 25 July 1999. It had come to Camberwell after Walworth closed on 2 November 1985 and stayed for life.

T 1129 (WDA 4T) was one of the five ex-West Midlands Titans acquired in 1984 and put to use on the 177 Express. It was the only one to pass to London Central, but on 20 August 1999 at Bank was being put to use on the Northern Line replacement operated under the number 133.

T 1120 (B120 WUV) was new to Bromley in November 1984 but in September 1989 transferred to Bexleyheath where it would remain until replaced by a new PVL in April 2000. On 6 August 1999 it is seen setting off from the 422's Bexleyheath stand on the long trip to North Greenwich.

Everyone knows the 1933 livery applied to T 66, but the London Central Travel scheme that **T 172** (CUL 172V) received in April 1998 was every bit as splendid. Elderly for a service Titan at London Central by this time, it was too good to waste as a trainer in this livery and was put to work on private hire and specials like this bingo contract, on which it is seen at Surrey Quays on 11 October 1999. Later still it was treated to all-over gold for the Queens' Golden Jubilee in 2002, and even after that was given full London Central livery of the time.

A new bus stand is being built at Crystal Palace as Peckham's **T 1111** (B111 WUV) sets off on 11 August 1999. This bus had spent its first year at Plumstead and then five years at Camberwell before coming here, and would be withdrawn in December 1999.

Buying as much time as they could for their Titans without buying more paint than they felt was necessary, London Central gave some of their dwindling number of Ts lower-deck repaints (featuring the new, darker skirt) in 2000. One was **T 1057** (257 CLT, ex-A57 THX), a Peckham bus since transferring from New Cross in January 1991 and seen at London Bridge Station on 21 November 2000. It would last until March 2002.

The unassuming 172, stripped of its genuine credentials as a trunk route first through its withdrawal south of Brockley Rise and then through its diversion to St Paul's rather than Liverpool Street, ended up being the last wholly-Titan route. On 11 August 1999 New Cross's **T 931** (A931 SYE), which would last until July 2001, loads at Liverpool Street.

Looking smart under a new coat of paint, **T 985** (A985 SYE) takes on passengers at Bexleyheath Broadway on 6 August 1999. This one had been around more than most in this age group, serving at Walworth, Camberwell and New Cross and then briefly loaned to First Capital before landing at Bexleyheath in January 1999.

The 133's summer augmentation is seen in the hands of **T 952** (A952 SYE) on 16 July 1999 in King William Street. Only recently transferred to Peckham, this bus was better known for its brief spell in Bexleybus blue and cream in 1989. It would transfer back to New Cross in October 1999 and finish there in May 2001.

On the New Cross share of the 89 is **T 970** (A970 SYE), again a recent transfer to its garage (July 1998, from Camberwell). In this case it would not last the decade out, being withdrawn in December 1999 after the loss of the 1 and sold shortly afterwards. On the afternoon of 6 August 1999 it is seen setting off from Bexleyheath Broadway.

As the Millennium came and went, London received a new landmark, the giant Ferris wheel known as the London Eye. On 7 May 2000 the 12 has had to be diverted away from Whitehall for some reason or other, so **T 1086** (B86 WUV) has been caught coming onto Northumberland Avenue with the Eye in sight. This Peckham bus had run the gamut of south-east London garages but would spend its last four years here, coming off in April 2002.

New Cross's 172 became the last Titan route by default, once the conversions to low-floor or losses of other routes left it on its own. Now carrying a yellow band atop its otherwise unchanged ex-LBL tapegrey, **T 1004** (A604 THV) is seen at the Elephant on 9 August 2000.

The 3 lost its Titans on 5 February 2000, but in this case it was due to the loss of the route to Connex Buses. In fact, Ts had been only secondary to the intended SPs, but the Spectras were less reliable than wished and Titans would invariably man most of the route on Sundays. On 12 January 2000 **T 1040** (A640 THV) is seen in Oxford Street; it would be converted to a trainer not long after this and last till 2003.

T 1075 (A75 THX) is in its last month of service when captured at Lewisham on 14 April 2000; one of the 55 PVLs into Bexleyheath would see it off.

T 1043 (A643 THV) spent most of its life at Peckham before a transfer in March 1998 took it to New Cross. On 27 August 2000, Carnival day, it is seen at Elgin Avenue.

After two years at Catford, **T 765** (OHV 765Y) settled at New Cross and on 16 January 2000 was working the Sunday OPO arm of the 36 through Victoria.

The construction of Canada Water's bus station allowed easy shots of 381s at the same spot in either direction of the route. In 1995, shortly after privatisation, London Central had taken nine Alexander Royale-bodied Volvo Olympians from dealer stock to reduce the 381's age profile a little bit, but that wasn't enough to eject Titans from the whole route; hence we see **T 1057** (257 CLT, ex-A57 THX) and **AV 7** (M87 MYM) on 25 March 2000. The Titan would last at Peckham until March 2002, and the Olympian not appreciably longer.

On 23 September 2000 at Victoria the last knockings of the Art Bus were in the hands of **T 1129** (WDA 4T). It was now settled at New Cross and would stay there until sale to Skylark Travel in April 2002.

Struggling desperately under its imposed fleet of single-doored Dennis Dart SLFs, the busy 345 accepted the occasional Titan with gratitude, and just such is **T 774** (OHV 774Y) at Camberwell on 18 April 2000. At this point in time the route was subject to maddeningly constant allocation changes, with Camberwell coming on on 5 February 2000 and then off again on 17 June, only to return on 30 September!

As London Central's Titans entered their teens, their appearance dwindled accordingly and eventually repaints were sanctioned, but only to the lower decks. Thus, when seen coming up to London Bridge Station on 17 October 2000, Peckham's **T 980** (A980 SYE) looks smart from the waist down, new livery and all, but actually drawing attention to its overall condition. Even so, the partial repaint bought this Titan the time it needed and it survived to be one of Peckham's last two on 4 March 2003.

Similar treatment was afforded to another Peckham Titan, **T 1086** (B86 WUV), seen on 6 November 2000 at the same spot but headed in the other direction. It had only been based here since the conversion of the 21 to NV had made it spare from New Cross, but would last until April 2002.

All but the first two years of the service career of **T 806** (OHV 806Y) had been spent at New Cross, but in December 1997 it was transferred to Bexleyheath. On 22 April 2000, a month before its withdrawal, it is setting off from the Market Place terminus.

The 35 had received NVs in 1997, but Titans continued to turn out for as long as they remained at Camberwell; **T 757** (OHV 757Y) had been transferred there from Bexleyheath in June 1986 and would spend the next thirteen years there, transferring to New Cross in April 2000 for one last year. On 23 January 2000 it is heading south through Camberwell Green.

Carrying no London Central logos and with a set of 'LEYLAND'/'TITAN' front badges from a batch far older, Bexleyheath's **T 870** (A870 SUL) las over at North Greenwich on 18 January 2000. Despite having come to Bexleyheath in January 1999 after a loan period with Capital Citybus this Titan was most closely associated with New Cross, having begun there, and indeed it would end there with a final spell between March 2000 and June 2001.

On 18 April 2000 **T 956** (A956 SUL) is seen at Camberwell Green on a Sunday OPO working of the 12. AVLs and NVs had become that day of the week's staple since their arrival at Camberwell, but the trusty Titan could still be counted upon until the end. Not long after this picture was taken, T 956 was turned into a trainer.

The twin generations of Titan and Metrobus were suddenly thin on the ground by 2000 as low-floor double-deckers belatedly flooded in to replace them. Route 172, seen in the capable hands of New Cross's recently-received **T 704** (OHV 704Y) became the last wholly Titan-operated route in the spring of 2001, while the 243 with Tottenham's **M 767** (KYV 767X) out of Arriva London North lost its Ms for DLAs over the summer of 2000. They are seen side-by-side at Waterloo on 17 October 2000.

T 939 (A939 SYE) was a lifelong Peckham bus, entering service in March 1984 and lasting there until February 2000. This shot, taken on the 5th at Crystal Palace, may therefore be on one of its last days, as AVLs were by then taking over the 63.

On 8 November 1997 the 21 was split in half, the southeastern section becoming 321 between New Cross and Foots Cray Tesco. Bexleyheath and New Cross shared it in varying proportions, and in 1998 it was converted from T to LDP operation, although Titans remained available to sub the Dart SLFs at both garages. On 22 April 2000 New Cross's **T 983** (A983 SYE) is in Lewisham town centre.

T 983 (A983 SYE) is seen again on another unusual working, in this case the 345, which was by 1998 also LDP-operated. The single-doored Dart SLFs struggled desperately and were often helped out by double-deckers, and that's what this bus is doing when sighted at Peckham on 14 April 2000. It had been transferred from Bexleyheath to New Cross in February and retained its previous garage's code.

Lewisham was a Titan hub right up until the last year, served by Catford, New Cross and Bexleyheath routes, but on 20 January 2001 the 185 was lost by Stagecoach Selkent to London Easylink. Titans kept going on the 89 even after its conversion to PVL in 2000, and Bexleyheath's T 1037 (A637 THV) was one to escape withdrawal at that point. On the afternoon of 14 April 2001 it is seen at Lewisham in the company of Volvo B7TL VP 151 (X151 FBB), and later in the year and into 2002 it would help out repeatedly at New Cross and even Camberwell.

Finally the 172 was converted from T to PVL operation, and Titan holdings at London Central after the spring of 2001 were solely for backup purposes. On 24 March 2000 New Cross's T 991 (A991 SYE) rounds Waterloo, but amazingly it managed to sidestep withdrawal when the 172 was converted, transferring to Camberwell in June 2001 and remaining in service for another eleven months.

T 946 (A946 SYE) took the honours of being one of the last four Titans in service at Bexleyheath, coming off on 18 March 2002 after a day as BX58 on the 229. But on 21 November 2001 it was woring BX10 on the 89 and is captured doing so at Lewisham. Bexleyheath by that time had taken to displaying its running numbers in the windscreen, so the traditional running-number holders had fallen into disuse; but that's no reason for 'BX' to have been applied twice!

On 10 September 2001 Peckham's **T 963** (A963 SYE) looks smart, at least from the waistrail down, as it circumnavigates the site of its old garage. A latecomer to Peckham (March 1998), it would nonetheless hold out there until 4 March 2003.

Bexleyheath's last four Titans inched into 2002; one of them was **T 1051** (A651 THV) seen at Sidcup Station on 14 April 2001.

T 1037 (A637 THV) was without regular work by the time PVLs had effectively removed Titans from Bexleyheath, so in October 2001 was sent to New Cross to help out as a crew bus on the 36. On the 24th of that month it is seen at Lewisham. After this task was done, it returned briefly to Bexleyheath to see out the Titan there for real and then worked briefly out of Camberwell garage before finally finishing out its life at New Cross in March 2002.

The three Titans with dot-matrix blind boxes lingered for a long time after Ts were otherwise expelled from Camberwell, and on 10 September 2001 at Peckham, **T 1005** (A605 THV) was one of them, working (since it was a Monday) with a conductor. It was withdrawn in March 2003.

On 6 July 2001 at Orpington **T 1062** (A62 THX) pays a visit to the 51, otherwise NV-operated since 1995. This bus was late into Bexleyheath, coming in October 1999 as a transfer from New Cross, but would stay until March 2002.

T 803 (OHV 803Y) became London Central's showpiece, combining its long-established open-top status with the application of the company's truly terrific special purposes livery. It is seen on the Cobham-Brooklands bus service during the rally of 8 April 2001, but had been put out on the 12 from time to time.

As Titan operation was coming to an end at New Cross, the garage put **T 991** (A991 SYE) out on the 171, otherwise the province of NVs and soon to be replaced themselves by PVLs from the same batch that was finishing off the 172's Ts at the time this picture was taken at the bottom of Brockley Rise on 5 May 2001. Even so, T 991 remained in use, transferring to Camberwell.

The career of **T 984** (A984 SYE), did, however, come to an end when the 172 was converted from T to PVL. A little before that commenced, it is seen at Aldwych on 13 March 2001.

Looking fine until you pan upwards from the waistline, Peckham's **T 1033** (A633 THV) lingered into 2002, lasting on the 381 and 63 until October of that year. On 18 September it is seen passing Waterloo.

Converted to a trainer in December 1997, **T 831** (A831 SUL) had spent its first two years at Catford and the next twelve at New Cross. Now it was in the hands of Bexleyheath, and on 21 March 2002 is entering Regent Street from Oxford Circus.

By the start of 2002 Titans at Camberwell were in single figures, three of which were the dot-matrix examples that had been on long-term standby to cover any night route when needed. Another one was **T 1018** (A618 THV), officially placed at Camberwell in February after a period of emergency loans to and from Blue Triangle, Peckham and New Cross. Most of its life had been spent at Peckham, as it happened, but in its final knockings with Camberwell it would eventually be given the honour of seeing the Titan out. For the moment, it is seen on 6 February 2002 at County Hall.

The last four Ts at Bexleyheath were participants in the last hurrah of the class there when new route 486 was introduced on 23 February. Aside from the MD-class DAFs inherited from the previous M1 route, PVLs, NVs and even two Ts were in evidence on the first day, and it doesn't matter too much that temporary blinds are all that **T 1062** (A62 THX) can muster when sighted leaving North Greenwich.

The late-afternoon time of day permitted better rear offside shots, and this one of the same Titan shows the absolutely appalling treatment it has been subjected to by its passengers, with not a pane of glass left unetched. At over seventeen years of age and without the benefit of an overhaul, this bus would have been a candidate for withdrawal anyway about now.

Peckham's **T 963** (A963 SYE) and T 980 were the last two Titans at their garage, both coming off service after 4 March 2003. On 10 September 2001 it is seen loading up at King's Cross.

T 1000 (ALM 1B, ex-A600 THV) was re-registered with this Routemaster mark as far back as 1987, but by 2002 was one of just five Titans left at Camberwell. On 24 April it is seen at Trafalgar Square.

The three dot-matrix Ts at Camberwell were put out most often in lieu of Routemasters on the 12, but there were a handful of other double-deck routes they could still visit, like the 45 as on 4 September 2002 in the hands of **T 1000** (ALM 1B, ex-A600 THV) at the Elephant.

T 172 (CUL 172V) was several years older than the run of London Central-inherited Titans, but its repaint into tramways livery in April 1998 secured not only its immortality, but the plain truth of a few more years in normal service. It looks magnificent, and why it couldn't have been a standard livery for one or all post-'London Transport' companies can only have been down to cost. It is seen arriving at Peckham on 15 January 2002.

Tramways livery wasn't even the end for **T 172** (CUL 172V), for in March 2002 it was given all-over gold for the Queen's Golden Jubilee. However, the effect was less memorable, due to the predominance of vinyl which didn't shine like the gold paint applied to the trickier areas, as seen in this Waterloo picture of 18 June.

Alone among the fifty Golden Jubilee buses, **T 172** (CUL 172V) included two black horizontal bands, perhaps for the Queen Mother, who had died at the start of the commemorations, or perhaps for the Titan as a whole, which was now down to fewer than twenty members. On 4 September 2002 it is taking a turn on the 63 at Elephant & Castle.

On 15 May 2002 Camberwell's **T 1005** (A605 THV) is passing roadworks in Trafalgar Square, but these are small beans beside what was about to happen to this key junction, which from 1 September was hacked apart so that the north side of the square could be pedestrianised. Massive tailbacks ensued in every possible direction, but at least it slowed down buses for the purposes of photography.

As 2003 opened there were just six Titans in service, and after the withdrawal of Peckham's pair in March, followed by the Camberwell dot-matrix examples, just **T 1018** (A618 THV) remained. It got to go around on its own for three months, and was spruced up with a partial repaint that turned its LBL tapegrey skirt to charcoal grey. Rostered mostly on the 12, but also turning out on the 35, 40 and 45, it is seen in Oxford Street on 25 March 2003.

And on to the last day, Thursday 19 June 2003. **T 1018** (A618 THV) was star for a day, but its ticket was about to expire so today was selected for it to see the Titan out on its own. It almost didn't make it that far, having been involved in multiple accidents in the last week alone, the most recent of which was in the garage and which necessitated a new windscreen! Anyway, the panic was over and it could now form up for Q98, its day-long duty on the 40. Aldgate is the location at midday.

The recent lower-deck repaint had been augmented by new London Central logos on the front (contrasting with the LBL-inherited unit logo still on the side). and an enthusiast-made placard for the windscreen, reading 'London's Last Titan'. **T 1018** (A618 THV) is reversing onto stand at Aldgate a couple of minutes after the previous photograph was taken.

T 1018 (A618 THV), seen from the offside aspect at Aldgate, had been around in its nineteen years, starting at Catford in April 1984 before transferring to Sidcup in September 1986 and then to New Cross on 16 January 1988, when Sidcup closed. It passed to Peckham in January 1991 and stayed a decade before its latter-day wanderings, but Camberwell was where it finished up. The 40 itself had only gravitated south of the river through the closure of Poplar on 2 November 1985; that garage's crew Ts were replaced by Camberwell OPO Ts two years newer. In the interim the southern terminus had switched from Herne Hill to Dulwich, the central part pulled back from Poplar to Blackwall and then to Aldgate and the vehicle complement updated so that NVs took over in 1997.

It is worth noting that the Routemaster outlived the Titan, two generations its junior, but even as **T 1018** (A618 THV) was captured arriving at Dulwich during the afternoon in the company of fellow Camberwell Routemaster **RML 2270** (CUV 270C), plans were being laid to remove the remaining Routemasters within two years.

The final journey of **T 1018** (A618 THV) was the 19:32 departure of Q98 from Dulwich Library to Aldgate, and that's what the enthusiasts are waiting for.

T 1018 (A618 THV) arrived at Aldgate at 20:32, let its passengers off, posed for photos and then set off home. Ensigns had already purchased it and been by to take it off to Purfleet, but had to wait until it had finished. It was subsequently sold to Blackburn Transport and lasted there at least a few years.

STAGECOACH EAST LONDON

On 13 April 1998 North Street's **T 12** (WYV 12T) is on its way through Romford town centre before the main slog westward to Stratford. Stagecoach East London at the start of the period covered by this book could field almost all of the first forty Titans, which were coming up to twenty years old but had outlasted a large number of far newer, ostensibly identical Titans. These Park Royals were considered substantially better than their all-Leyland siblings and indeed would endure all the way to the end of Titan operation at Stagecoach East London in the autumn of 2001.

From the middle order is a Titan that's not quite Park Royal and not quite Leyland, as it was one of the thirteen constructed by the latter from parts still existing when the former was closed down. Leyton's **T 262** (GYE 262W), seen at Walthamstow Central on 13 June 1998, had actually come from Catford four months earlier, as revealed by the Stagecoach Selkent fleetnames and amateurishly-corrected garage code. It was withdrawn in December 1999.

Somebody ought to tell the driver of Barking's **T 434** (KYV 434X) that his bus's blind box has fallen open. Despite having been pulled further and further out of the City of London, the 5 could still boast a Sunday extension as far as Old Street and that is what T 434 is performing as it pulls away from Liverpool Street on 19 April 1998. This bus was fairly recent to Barking, but would end its career there in June 2001.

Although its pretensions beyond Ilford had been pegged back in recent years, the 25 was still a powerful force out to east London and by 1997 had been converted from Titan to Volvo Olympian operation, first VNs and then VAs. However, Bow continued to put Titans out as long as it had them, and on 22 May 1998 in New Oxford Street we see **T 340** (KYV 340X). This Titan had just completed ten years with Bow, ever since coming for the 25's OPO conversion on 16 January 1988, and would finish from there in December 1999.

High numbered for a Bow Titan, **T 996** (A996 SYE) stages through Tower Hill on 17 May 1998. It had come to Bow from Catford the previous December, but its relative newness would not save it from withdrawal as early as August 1998.

By the spring of 1998 Leyton was busy replacing its Titans on the 48 55 and 56 with a slew of long-wheelbase Volvo Olympians of both VA and VN classes. **T 473** (KYV 473X) stayed put during this conversion, being seen on 26 May 1998 in Oxford Street, but would leave for North Street in April 1999 and spend a final year there.

The 58 had been rerouted in 1988 to terminate at Walthamstow Central, while 1993 had seen its other end pointed to East Ham rather than Canning Town. **T 498** (KYV 498X) was brought north from Bromley in February 1998, and on 28 June is seen in Walthamstow Central bus station as a Leyton bus. It would linger here until October 2000, when the 58 was converted to TA operation.

On 3 June 1998 **T 545** (KYV 545X) is seen on the 25 in Oxford Street; although just transferred to Bow, it is still carrying the North Street code from whence it came. Its time at Bow would be short, as it was transferred to Catford in April 1999 and can be seen operating from that garage elsewhere in this book.

The 56 was created out of the severed ends of the 277 and 38 and has been run by Leyton ever since. The first eight years saw Titan operation from the likes of **T 541** (KYV 541X), caught at Clapton Pond on 7 June 1998, but this was to be its last month here as it departed for Catford, replaced by a Volvo Olympian.

Early to the Titan, Barking had operated very large numbers since, though a complete rotation in 1991/92 had taken out all the original V-registered examples and replaced them with newer ones. **T 603** (NUW 603Y) had served at Barking before, at the end of 1991, but had moved on again, only to return in December 1996 and spent until April 1999 there, after which it was transferred to Catford. It is seen at Barking station on 12 April 1998.

Caught in Oxford Street on 17 September 1998, **T 501** (KYV 501X) was on its second tour at Bow, though it had only been away from its first one for three months. When additional TAs came to Bow in March 1999, it was transferred to Catford, where it had spent part of the interregnum between its spells at Bow.

Bow was the final posting for **T 268** (GYE 268W), seen in Oxford Street on 14 July 1998, but over the previous seventeen years it had served at Upton Park, Plumstead, Ash Grove, Leyton, Walthamstow, Stamford Hill, West Ham, Upton Park (again) and Seven Kings. It was withdrawn in December 1999 and sold six months later to MASS.

The stop at the southern end of the Narroway in Hackney Central was an easy photographic pitch, everything coming through here on its way south or east. **T 640** (NUW 640Y) on the 55 on 19 April 1998 was one such capture, though the black-painted garage code holder was evidence that this bus was meant to stick to the 30, which was running experimental observation software at the time. This bus was about to leave, heading for Bromley in June.

T 260 (GYE 260W) was coming to the end of a productive two decades, starting at Upton Park and then working out of Seven Kings, Barking, Upton Park (again), Leyton and Catford before coming back to Leyton in February 1998 when the 55 was taken back. This would be its last posting, but before that it is seen at Leyton station on 9 September 1998.

When sighted at Walthamstow Central on 13 June 1998, T 804 (OHV 804Y) is still wearing Catford codes after over fourteen years based there, but as of February 1998 it was now a Leyton bus. It would return to Selkent in July, first to Bromley, then back at Catford and finally to Bromley again to finish its career.

Seen at the same stand but taken from the reverse angle, Leyton's T 749 (OHV 749Y) has had some heavy repanelling that just needs the final touch of the paintbrush before being good as new, but there's no need to deprive the passengers of a bus just because it's not picture-perfect. This bus had been based at Leyton since February 1990, but when replaced by a VA or VN in June would move south, taking up at Bromley and then Catford.

Winter is setting in in Barking on 5 November 1998, sufficient for North Street's **T 543** (KYV 543X) to have to have a piece of cardboard inserted under its air intake. By coincidence, **T 544** (KYV 544X) is coming up behind, but that's a Barking bus.

Like many of us in midlife, **T 193** (CUL 193V) felt compelled to wander after its early period of stability, which in its own case was spent at Barking. However, in 1992 Barking was upgrading with newer Titans and T 193 moved on. On 9 September 1998 it was part of Leyton's fleet and is seen at the Underground station of that name, but one last move would take it to North Street to finish out its life.

This spot at Barking station was often impeded by taxis and cars dropping off until it was filled in. **T 458** (KYV 458X) had come to Barking in April 1998 after a decade at Bow and is seen on 1 August. It would last until the end of Titans at Barking in June 2001.

Leyton's **T 590** (NUW 590Y) is amid unlovely surroundings at Dalston Junction, a decade before the London Overground was envisaged in this sector. To its credit, the shop behind did a roaring trade in blank tapes, found useful by the author! It's 5 September 1998 in this picture and T 590 was based at only its second garage, having spent its first ten years at West Ham and transferring to Leyton when it closed.

Only two Titans were fitted with this style of rear lights to replace their factory-fitted BMAC 343 arrays. This is **T 521** (KYV 521X) out of Leyton, seen at the 230's Wood Green stand on 22 August 1998 and deputising for a Dart SLF that couldn't make it and which was, in any case, too small for this busy route.

Stratford's only Titan-operated route was the 30, operation of which had bounced around the local garages in the decade since OPO conversion before settling here. **T 360** (KYV 360X) wears the black running-number holder denoting buses fitted with tracking equipment for this route, and on 25 July 1998 is seen in Dalston. It was withdrawn in July 2000.

Upton Park had long discarded its Titans for VNs, but a small number remained behind as dual-purpose trainers and service buses. **T 971** (A971 SYE) was one of them, and on 31 August 1998 is on a Bank Holiday Monday OPO working on the 15 at Charing Cross.

T 631 (NUW 631Y) is missing its light cluster panels when seen at Barking on 5 November 1998. It would leave Barking garage when the 5 was converted to TA in May 1999.

The 30 lingered into 2001 with T operation, **T 617** (NUW 617Y) being the last at Stratford. Amid Christmas decorations on 11 December 1998 it has dawdled sufficient for **T 559** (NUW 559Y) to close up to it in Mare Street.

On 5 November 1998 Barking's **T 650** (NUW 650Y) has nearly finished its journey from Romford. The 87 went much further before 4 September 1982, the hairpin to Rainham passing to the modern 287, which indeed, outlived its parent. T 650 spent only two and a bit years at Barking, heading east to North Street in April 1999 and finishing its life at Catford two years and five months later.

A typically long-stayer in its age group, **T 15** (WYV 15T) differed from the usual Hornchurch-to-North Street progression of its siblings in that it served at other garages, albeit briefly; these were Barking immediately after overhaul and Leyton a year before the end of its life. On 24 June 1999 it is seen at Romford station.

As late as 9 September 1998 Barking's **T 637** (NUW 637Y) has still got its LBL tape relief band, and its original *EAST LONDON* front logo had lasted into this year as well. Replaced at Barking by a TA coming in for the 5, this bus moved to Catford in April 1999 and spent the rest of that year there before withdrawal.

North Street's **T 163** (CUL 163V), seen at Romford on 26 June 1999, had served at North Street before, between September 1982 and December 1983, but that was far in the past now, with Stagecoach East London now in ownership. Most of its life was spent at Barking, but its second spell at North Street came after transferring from Catford in October 1995. It would be withdrawn in February 2000 and sold that July to MASS.

T 260 (GYE 260W) finds itself working out of Leyton for a second time when seen at Wood Green on 5 March 1999, but the 230 wasn't a Titan route; it was meant for SLDs, but there weren't enough of them and the ones that did turn out ended up full from the first stop outbound. It was withdrawn in November and sent off to Stagecoach East Kent.

On 22 March 1999 **T 28** (WYV 28T) is part-way through a route 175 journey at Romford. Having served at just Hornchurch and North Street, it was withdrawn in September 2001.

From lacking Titans until 1987, Leyton amassed a large fleet of them to furnish the busy routes in this part of north-east London, and the garage's role increased when Walthamstow closed on 23 November 1991. **T 447** (KYV 447X) and **T 439** (KYV 439X) are manoeuvring themselves past a Grey-Green Dart SLF on the 20 within Walthamstow Central on 5 March 1999. T 447 went to Catford but came back to Leyton to finish in December 2000, whilst T 439 also made the move south, there to finish in June 2000.

North Street's **T 21** (WYV 21T) had managed to keep hold of its foglights when captured at Romford on 21 April 1999, but its upper-deck opening windows were long gone. Having gone through the usual progression of ten years at Hornchurch and thirteen at North Street, T 21 was to be the last in service on 7 September 2001, along with T 1 and straggler T 537 from a higher batch.

The only other Titan with an S-registration, **T 2** (THX 402S) had passed its 20th birthday in service by the time it was snapped at Romford on 21 April 1999, and it still had two years left in it.

The school routes in and around the Romford area were particularly well patronised, and the 649 could muster three Titans, one of which on 22 March 1999 was **T 33** (WYV 33T). After withdrawal in September 2001, it would stay in the area as a Blue Triangle bus.

Never kept in cotton wool despite its low number, **T 1** (THX 401S) remained in daily service for nearly twenty-three years alongside its much-prized Park Royal siblings, first from Hornchurch and then North Street. On 2 September 1999, on a route that had otherwise converted to Volvo Olympians during 1997, it rounds Ilford's complicated one-way system on its way east.

Inching its way along the otherwise pedestrianised bottom section of East Ham High Street on 16 May 1999 is Barking's **T 564** (NUW 564Y). The 238 had remained with Titan operation from when Upton Park first received the type in 1981, but the latter-day Barking operation had been cut back to Barking garage and converted to Dart operation. That is, however, until Ts returned on 19 July 1997. Titan operation on the route would end for good on 19 October 1999 when Upton Park resumed control, this time with Scanias. T 564 itself continued on at Barking until June 2001.

The Leyland badge is offset too far to the nearside on Barking's **T 597** (NUW 597Y) in this 24 June 1999 shot. The 169 had also been taken out of consideration for Titan operation during the 1990s, but in this case it accepted Optare Deltas and thus T 597 is a strange visitor. It too lasted until June 2001.

North Street's **T 12** (WYV 12T) heads through Clements Road in Ilford on 2 September 1999, a decade before extensive construction would alter the background in this otherwise rather forgotten southern bit of Ilford. This bus survived until September 2001 and was sold to Blue Triangle for a bit more action in this part of town.

The sheer upheaval to London's buses in the 1980s and 1990s disrupted the traditional orderly replacement of one type of bus with another, so much so that Titans had no natural predators as such. Olympians didn't come to this sector with LBL and tendering losses locally only thinned Titan numbers rather than gutted them. Scanias, meanwhile, were so few in number around here that they never threatened the Titan. But then came the Volvo Olympian, already standard in Stagecoach and easily adapted to London's needs. Thus on 22 October 1999 at Romford station we see **T 2** (THX 402S) flanked by **VN 120** (R120 XNO) and **VN 30** (P530 HMP). In the end, however, the Titan would complete 22 years in service, whereas the two VNs would both be gone by 2003, victims of the politically-correct but extremely wasteful drive towards low-floor operation.

T 230 (EYE 230V) was one of the pack of ageing Titans that roved between Stagecoach East London and Stagecoach Selkent garages filling in where needed and then moving on again. When seen at Walthamstow Central on 31 July 1999 in the company of fellow Leyton bus T 498 (KYV 498X), somehow it's acquired itself a roof dome off an Olympian.

The 247 was one of those routes that looked ripe for demotion to minibus (as indeed took place in 1993), but loadings remained just too much for Darts to handle, however big each generation kept getting, and nor could the miscellany that Stagecoach brought down soon after taking over. Thus, Titans remained available for use and here at Romford on 22 October 1999 is T 214 (CUL 214V), another of the wandering pack of standby Titans. It had just come to North Street and would finish from there in February 2000.

A more stable Leyton Titan route by far was the 56, created in 1990 and keeping Ts for eight years despite assistance from Ss at one point. On 4 August 1999 at the Angel T 437 (KYV 437X) is visiting from the 58, the 56 having otherwise been converted to VA/VN operation and then to TAs from the first big batch of Tridents. T 437 would leave for Catford in January 2000 and finish its career there three months later, although it did spend six more months as a trainer before final sale.

On 26 June 1999 the 262 and 473 were put into Bow to make up for that garage's loss of the 25, and immediately Titans started appearing. Coming into Stratford's bus station on 13 November is **T 366** (KYV 366X), which since September had actually been a Stratford bus. This would be its last hurrah in service, as withdrawal came at the end of the year.

During 1999 the Stratford-based Titans on the 30 had route branding applied on behalf of Sadler's Wells Theatre. This was a stretch, as the closest the route got was about half a mile away at the Angel. This is **T 467** (KYV 467X), seen at Hackney on 21 November 1999 and coming to the end of its career.

We crossed into the new millennium with slightly over 300 Titans still in service between London Central and Stagecoach's two firms, but in a year that would have halved as low-floors swept in. The 247 had long since ceased to be a Titan route, the latest set of single-deckers to be specified being Plaxton-bodied Dart SLFs, but on 18 January 2000 at Romford we see **T 35** (WYV 35T) paying a visit.

The 58 became Leyton's last Titan route, lasting until the start of 2001, and on 13 January 2000 at Walthamstow Central, **T 581** (NUW 581Y) reposes. It had come to Leyton in June 1999 and would finish its career there, but not without a full repaint right at the death.

By the turn of the century, Titans at North Street formed the standard allocation on the 174, 175 and 296 (with the 496 to follow), but more often than not they would visit routes since converted to newer buses. The 374 was one such, since 1997 in the hands of single-doored VNs but rather better served by buses like **T 33** (WYV 33T), seen coming into Romford on 24 May 2000.

T 2 (THX 402S) looks spry when captured at Romford station on 26 February 2000, but the black paint on the grille's been added incorrectly over the panel edges. No matter; this bus would soldier on all the way to the end of Titan operation at North Street, with a few special appearances planned for later in the year.

Still T-operated as the century opened, the 294 had been that way for over twenty years, although back then **T 1** (THX 401S) was based at nearby Hornchurch. The 294 was actually intended for conversion to TA at this point, but the new Tridents failed clearance tests so were redeployed to the 86. T 1 looks weary, but it would soon be repainted back into its 1978 livery to give the class some glamour with which to see out its days.

T 627 (NUW 627Y) had been transferred from Stratford to Leyton when the 30 was converted to TA in February 2000, but this was to be its last shot, as it was withdrawn in June. On 26 February it is on its way to its new base after a route 58 duty to Walthamstow Central.

Touched up around the front and needing Stagecoach East London insignia reapplied when sighted at Romford on 20 May 2000 is North Street's **T 18** (WYV 18T).

For three years or so, the message of low-floor wheelcair accessibility could only be accomplished with single-deckers, leading to some extremely crowded routes like the 230, which received service increase after service increase but never improved. Even so, the need to keep sticking out Titans on the 230 in lieu of its SLDs cost everyone on those particular instances the chance to get beyond Whipps Cross to Upper Walthamstow, which could not, as yet, handle double-deckers. **T 498** (KYV 498X) spent between February 1998 and October 2000 at Leyton, and on 21 August it is seen on stand at Wood Green.

T 512 (KYV 512X) was the Titan that wouldn't die, being variously burned and then drowned. After the arson incident that cost it its upper deck in 1988, it was converted to open-top format and became a stalwart around east London. On 18 March 2000 it is seen carrying some revellers around Aldgate while on attachment to Upton Park.

By 6 April 2000, when this picture of **T 525** (KYV 525X) was taken at Ilford, Barking garage could field 23 Titans for the 87 and 387. That's why one of them's on the 169! Based here since March 1993, T 525 would come off in June 2001 when TAs arrived.

T 525 (KYV 525X) is seen again, this time with its closest sibling T 526 (KYV 526X) at Romford on 26 February 2000. They finished at the same garage (Barking), having arrived there in March 2003 after widely disparate careers which took in the likes of Chalk Farm and Kingston (T 525) and Croydon and Catford (T 526).

T 471 (KYV 471X) spent six years at North Street, nine years at Bow and the winter of 1997/98 at Bromley before pitching up at Leyton, where it would spend the rest of its life. It is seen departing from Walthamstow Central on 29 April 2000.

A journeyman among Titans, T 306 (KYN 306X) had two six-year spells at one garage (Bow between 1988 and 1994 and North Street between 1994 and 2000) but nowhere longer. On 1 August 2000 it is seen at Romford, still carrying its foglights, but it would move to Barking for the last knockings of its career. It is now in preservation.

Outlasting both Scanias and Volvo Olympians at Leyton, Titans continued until the beginning of 2001 and were still able to creep out on the 55 when a TA could not be persuaded. That's what **T 539** (KYV 539X) is doing on 4 May 2000 at Tottenham Court Road. It was at its last garage after a succession of short spells taking in Clapton, Walthamstow, West Ham, Clapton again, Ash Grove, West Ham again and Barking, and withdrawal would ensue in December 2000.

So that's why the Leyland badge was all the way over there on Barking's **T 597** (NUW 597Y). Plastering a vinyl sticker over the front can't have been much of a help sealing in heat, however; sealing in adhesive with the accompanying smell will have been more likely. See how it turned out on the opposite page, but for now here it is at Romford on 26 Febrary 2000.

Credit to North Street's engineers for keeping in service what were by now very obsolete buses, almost all of which were over 21 years old by 2000, but which were considered far better than the all-Leyland Titans that came after. **T 8** (WYV 8T) has needed a new front panel for a trip to the 374 on 24 May.

At the very close of its career **T 631** (NUW 631Y) benefited from a repaint, albeit another one going over the edges of the radiator grille in black. This Titan too had roved all over the map, racking up two separate phases at Clapton and three at Barking before settling finally at Leyton and the 58. Walthamstow Central is where it is seen on 25 March 2000.

On 8 December 2000, nine months after its previous depiction here (see facing page), **T 597** (NUW 597Y) now has a new front with no badges at all, and that was how it would finish out its days at Barking in June 2001.

Smartly repainted for the final stages of North Street Titan operation is **T 8** (WYV 8T), seen at Romford on 26 February 2000, but it would need a new offside corner panel within two months (see facing page).

Another late-career repaint, at least partially so (including overpainted grille edges), **T 28** (WYV 28T) out of North Street works through Romford on 4 March 2001.

Conversely, North Street stablemate **T 21** (WYV 21T) looks tired all round, with new (and mismatched) bumper) and paint coming off the roof, but it would end up being the last in service alongside T 1. It's 22 July 2001 and the location is Romford station.

The bumper mismatch is on the other side with **T 12** (WYV 12T) on 6 July. TAS arrival was imminent now and the Titans were on borrowed time.

As the summer of 2001 got going, Barking's Titans were withdrawn in droves as the new TAs for the 87 and 387 were delivered. Probably the very last London Titan able to blaze its foglights was **T 306** (KYN 306X), seen at Barking on 24 March 2001, shortly after transferring from North Street to Barking garage.

North Street's **T 12** (WYV 12T) and **T 21** (WYV 21T) in Romford on 22 July 2001 show off the most common alteration to the classic Titan rear, the flush-fitting rear light clusters.

Barking's **T 454** (KYV 454X) passes through Ilford on 24 March 2001. It had been based here since the end of 1996, plus one brief loan to Leyton, but was withdrawn in July 2001.

After ten years at West Ham, **T 465** (KYV 465X) led an unsettled sort of life, serving at Upton Park, Barking and North Street before drifting back to Barking in April 1995. It is seen at Barking station on 24 March 2001, three months before withdrawal.

The 5 had been the first Barking Titan route to fall to TAs, in 1999, but as long as they were still around, Ts continued to appear right up to the end. On 3 June at Barking, **T 537** (KYV 537X) passes **TA 77** (T677 KPU). As it turned out, the 5 would spend eighteen years with TAs, rotating its early examples in 2003 and only losing them when the route (by now having swallowed up the 87) passed to Blue Triangle.

Holding out on its own into 2001 at Stratford, **T 617** (NUW 617Y) shows the new and less attractive way of displaying the 30's running numbers when caught in Mare Street on 5 January 2001.

T 517 (KYV 517X) was withdrawn in June 2001, but on 24 March was still putting in work; not on its proper 87 or 387, but the 169 at Barking!

Time is ticking down on the career of **T 504** (KYV 504X) as it rounds the Barking town centre hairpin on 24 March 2001, but this would not actually be its final posting; when displaced by a Y-reg TA in June it would transfer to North Street and last two more months.

This page shows the final year of Barking Titan operation. On the other side of the fiddly hairpin that took buses away from the shopping streets in which they are most needed is **T 583** (NUW 583Y) on 24 March 2001. This bus had actually started south of the river, at Walworth, but came to east London garages in 1984 and stayed in that half of town ever since. Barking, from December 1996 to June 2001, was its last posting.

The last Titan in service at Barking was **T 568** (NUW 568Y), not reported after 13 August 2001. On 3 June it was operating Barking's Sunday-only share of the 147 through Ilford.

T 828 (A828 SUL) was a very high number for Barking, and indeed had spent all seventeen years and seven months of its career at Catford before crossing the river for one last throw in March 2001. Seen coming through Ilford on 7 May, it was withdrawn in June.

One coming, one going, but both would be going within weeks of this Barking station photograph taken on 3 June 2001. **T 578** (NUW 578Y) had turned in nine years at Barking, but **T 460** (KYV 460X) had only come in February, despite having worked at Barking before, during 1993.

The first Y-reg Titan, **T 550** (NUW 550Y) was a late transfer from Barking to North Street in June 2001. Before its nine years at Barking, it had had a varied career encompassing service at Sidcup, Plumstead, Chalk Farm, Muswell Hill, Finchley, Croydon and Catford. Seen on 22 July 2001 at Romford, it would come off in August, before the mass of T-reg Park Royals.

STAGECOACH SELKENT

As soon as they'd acquired Selkent from London Buses Ltd, Stagecoach wasted no time getting rid of the grey skirts, one of its less memorable features and absolutely impractical on an area of the bus subject to the most damage and resultant need for repainting. **T 830** (A830 SUL) was a Catford lifer, and on 11 September 1998 shows off its half-and-half livery in Lewisham High Street.

Full repaints followed at a breakneck pace, although into all red rather than the white and stripes for which Stagecoach was well known (or notorious, take your pick). **T 877** (A877 SUL), Leyland TL11-engined and rather bounced around the garages before acquiring a bit of stability at Bromley since November 1989, was treated in September 1995. At Selkent, the fleetnumbers were taken off the sides (leaving nothing visible there at all) and relocated to the front, although the 'London Transport Bus Service' sticker covers one of them. Seen passing through East Croydon on 10 April 1998, T 877 was subsequently re-engined with a Gardner unit and lasted at Bromley until October 2000, when it crossed the river to become a trainer at Leyton for one last year.

The first of the seven 'Rickys', **T 816** (RYK 816Y) is also resplendent in all-over red when seen in Lewisham High Street on 28 April 1998. As well as the fleetnumber on the front, Stagecoach Selkent differered from established London Transport practice (as well as that of its East London sibling) in not displaying the garage codes. This one, however, is based out of Catford, as were most buses running through this thoroughfare. Indeed not serving from anywhere else, it was repainted in October 1996 and lasted until March 2001.

The 47 would spend seventeen years with Titans, the first two of them crew-operated. Also on 24 May 1998 but in Lewisham High Street we see Catford's **T 834** (A834 SUL), there since new and not to operate from anywhere else, though it was a comparatively early withdrawal in July 1999.

Tendering had progressively drawn routes further away from practically-sited garages as more and more distant operators took a punt on them, and the 320 was no different. Carved out of the old Country Area 410, it was reassigned from London & Country to Stagecoach Selkent on 8 November 1997 and put into Bromley in a swap with the 198. **T 740** (OHV 740Y) is waiting for the off at Bromley North on 22 April 1998, but would be transferred to Catford in November and spend two and a half more years there.

The saga of the 60 was a cautionary tale in multiple parts, beginning on 29 August 1998 with the turning over of most of the route to Stagecoach Selkent, whose Bromley garage was perennially under-used. At first only temporary blinds could be mustered, as on **T 880** (A880 SUL) in Croydon on the first day, but **T 961** (A961 SYE) could manage a full set, and later, on 11 September, **T 640** (NUW 640Y) has come south from Leyton and still carries its East London fleetnames. Bromley would have to step aside on 23 January 1999, when Selkent was able to fill its gaps with plenty of new work, but all hell promptly broke loose when the intended contractor choked at the last minute and the second in line was nowhere near ready to take their place.

T 10 (WYV 10T) was the lowest-numbered Titan to venture south of the river, coming to Catford from North Street in July 1996 and being captured having arrived at Lewisham on 6 August 1999. The 75 was more properly VN-operated at this point, but one of the 1997-vintage Volvo Olympians must not have been available.

Since its introduction in 1991 as the third incarnation of the number along the Lewisham-Catford corridor, the 199 had been operated by Catford Ts and taken them into the Stagecoach Selkent era with repaints evident on both T 1030 (A630 THV) and T 749 (OHV 749Y) at the southern end of Tower Bridge Road on 4 January 1999. This section would be abandoned when the planners anticipated, incorrectly as it turned out, that the forthcoming Jubilee Line Extension would be sufficient.

The demotion of several south-east London area Titan routes to minibus at the turn of the 1990s still left a need for double-deckers at school times, and some of these routes grew so busy as to require almost as many buses again. Renumbered from 338 into a dedicated series in the six hundreds, the 638 by 15 July 1999 required three Bromley Titans, and at Bromley South we see T 772 (OHV 772Y).

T 406 (KYV 406X) served at a whopping nine garages during its eighteen-year career as a London bus, but its spell at Catford between September 1999 and September 2000 marked the only time it would be based south of the river. Seen on 12 December 1999 at Lewisham, it still has its East London fleetnames and would need them again when it transferred to Barking.

On 6 August 1999 Catford's **T 38** (WYV 38T) heads south through Lewisham High Street. It had come here from North Street in November 1996 and would remain for the rest of its life, other than a short loan to London Easylink for the 185 while that company's own Volvo B7TLs were awaited.

The L-class Leyland Olympians may have been newer and thus ticked boxes where age constraints came into consideration, but there were more Titans and thus the older, purer London Transport design prevailed in the end. Ls had come to Catford in 1995 when Plumstead dispensed with large numbers of them, but **L 97** (C97 CHM) would be gone eighteen months before **T 529** (KYV 529X), formerly of Bow, was finished. Both are pictured at Shoreditch on 6 May 1999.

After the flurry of one-way systems constructed around town centres in the 1960s and 1970s, tentative moves were made towards restoring through traffic two decades later, beginning with buses. In this way a contraflow was created at Catford so that southbound buses would not have to waste time circumnavigating Rushey Green, and on 11 August 1999 **T 1036** (A636 THV) is seen in the new red asphalt. It had just been transferred from Catford, but the garage code had not been fully amended from 'TL' to 'TB'. After a year here it would pass to Barking for training work before sale in August 2001.

Another Catford Titan with the squashed-number blind set, **T 614** (NUW 614Y) was another transfer from Barking, displaced by new Tridents onto the 5. Catford was where it would spend the rest of its life, albeit including a loan to London Easylink in January 2001, but for now it is seen at Catford on 31 May 1999.

Another Barking Titan displaced to Catford by TAs during April 1999, **T 653** (NUW 653Y) climbs Tooley Street towards London Bridge on 20 August. This bus would also finish its career at Catford, topping it off with a loan to London Easylink.

At the town end of the 47, **T 770** (OHV 770Y) has just come past Liverpool Street on 6 May 1999 and is on the home stretch. This is its second tour of duty at Catford, but even after its withdrawal from there in March 2001 a need was identified for it at North Street for four more months.

A lifelong Catford bus, 'Ricky' **T 818** (RYK 818Y) is seen in Lewisham High Street on the 199; it's 17 April 1999 but the turn of the century would see TAs taking over that route. Nonetheless, it lasted until March 2001.

With a headlight surround panel needing a bit of touching up in black, **T 548** (KYV 548X) comes into the bus station at Surrey Quays Shopping Centre during the afternoon of 18 May 2000. It had come to Catford when TAs displaced it from the 277 at Bow and would stay until March 2001.

The 'next generation' of buses had their introduction postponed by a decade due to the upheaval of privatisation, but by the second half of the 1990s the Volvo Olympian was entering service in large numbers, funded by corporate money the likes of which LBL had never been able to muster at the end of its existence. On 14 October 2000 in Bromley town centre, **T 1003** (A603 THV) is joined by **VA 127** (R127 EVX).

Despite its blind's route number being condensed almost to invisibility, **T 37** (WYV 37T) represents a better option on the 160 than the huge variety of single-deckers that had operated on it before and after its extension from Eltham over the old 228 to Sidcup. On 4 March 2000 it is coming up to the War Memorial at Chislehurst.

One with fixed upper-deck glass and the other with openers, but neither with foglights, **T 1065** (A65 THX) and **T 925** (A925 SYE) at Lewisham on 23 June 2000 represent the final form of the Leyland Titan with Stagecoach Selkent. Compare the blinds also, with the full 208 on T 1065 but T 925 making do with the northern section. Both buses were weeks away from withdrawal.

Looking rough with panels in primer and the obligatory patching of the nearside roof dome against tree damage, Catford's **T 19** (WYV 19T) swings past roadworks at London Bridge on 29 September 2000. It would be withdrawn in December.

In the spot where Peckham garage was until 1993, **T 521** (KYV 521X) reverses onto stand on 4 August 2000, beside 'one-eyed' **T 815** (OHV 815Y) ready to depart. The consolidation of Selkent under the management of East London led to the positioning of fleetnames and fleetnumbers according to the latter's practice, but despite having been transferred to Catford from North Street the previous November, T 521 carries no fleetnames at all. It was withdrawn in March 2001, just after Catford lifer T 815.

Titans may have been criticised upon their introduction for their oversophistication, but it worked for them; no other modern bus will manage up to 23 years in everyday frontline service. That said, **T 529** (KYV 529X) from the less-favoured middle order of all-Leyland-built examples (despite its earlier grille with British Leyland roundel), has had a bit of angle iron bolted on to prevent its front assembly from coming off in action. It is seen on 13 October 2000 at London Bridge, four months before withdrawal.

Catford's **T 26** (WYV 26T) has arrived at Peckham on 4 August 2000 and is swinging round onto stand. This too has managed to keep hold of its original grille badge after over 21 years in traffic though the foglights are gone and new flush bumpers fitted. It would be withdrawn in December 2000 but spent two more months in service from Bromley.

T 548 (KYV 548X) was one of nine Titans transferred from Bow to Catford in March 1999, and on 22 April 2000 is seen at the Catford end of Lewisham High Street. It would last at Catford until March 2001.

The conversion of Barking's 5 from T to TA made spare another batch of Titans, and **T 600** (NUW 600Y) came south to Catford in April 1999 with a group of eleven, though by the time this picture was taken in Lewisham on 22 April 2000, it hadn't had its East London logos replaced by correct Selkent ones.

T 600 (NUW 600Y) is seen again on 23 June 2000, this time on the 185, whose treatment on this notorious set of blinds hasn't been as severe as some of Catford's other routes. It was sold in December 2000.

The opening of the Jubilee Line extension forced the 199 to fall back from the Elephant & Castle to Canada Water, not only putting undue pressure on the 1 but obliging the stripping of the first two via points from the relevant Catford Titan blind. **T 533** (KYV 533X), only based here since February 1999, demonstrates on 23 January 2000 at Lewisham.

Covered with graffiti, **T 445** (KYV 445X) comes through a forest of cones at London Bridge on 10 July 2000. This bus had come south from Bow in April 1999 and would survive until March 2001.

T 650 (NUW 650Y) is away from the 185's usual starting point at Victoria on 16 January 2000 and has had to be diverted through the bus station. This was a new entrant to Catford, coming from North Street the previous month and managing nearly two years at its new base (including a loan to London Easylink in January 2001).

To commemorate the impending end of Titans at Bromley garage as well as encouraging donations to the British Legion Poppy Appeal, **T 2** (THX 402S) was borrowed from North Street on 11 September 2000 to run on four of its routes. In the afternoon it is seen setting off from Lewisham on the 208, with poppies clearly visible.

On 17 March 2000 **T 625** (NUW 625Y) finds itself at the 185's proper first outbound stop at Victoria. Yet another refugee from Stagecoach East London in the spring of 1999, this one had however come from Upton Park, and would last at Catford until February 2001.

The 199 had been converted from T to TA operation at the end of December 1999, as proved by what's behind **T 653** (NUW 653Y) in Lewisham High Street on 2 December 2000, but the 136 had a little while to go yet, and it was with the conversion of that route in February 2001 that this bus was stood down, having got the 185 started at London Easylink for its last duties.

A decade and a half since its most memorable career moment as the 1933-liveried *Aldenham Diplomat*, **T 66** (WYV 66T) could still be found in service as the 21st century commenced, though based at Catford since October 1996. On 16 August 2000 it is seen at Bermondsey heading towards town, with Canary Wharf and its growing siblings in the background. After a posting to London Easylink to bed in that company's acquisition of the 185, it was withdrawn in February 2001. Today in preservation it has returned to its splendid Golden Jubilee livery.

On 2 June 2000 Bromley's **T 804** (OHV 804Y) reposes at the 162's Beckenham Junction terminus. Although created for single-deckers and operated with Darts for the four years Kentish Bus had the route, the 162 was transferred to Stagecoach Selkent, which could only field Titans at that point. Eventually Dart SLFs were ordered for it, but T 804 was withdrawn before that happened.

With a new set of blinds reflecting the fact that the 199 went no further towards town than Canada Water, Catford's **T 805** (OHV 805Y) heads through Greenwich on 13 June 2000. Other than a brief loan to Camberwell in 1992, this bus served at Catford all its life and was withdrawn in March 2001.

T 805 (OHV 805Y) is seen again, this time crossing London Bridge on 25 July 2000. The 47 would end up being the last T-operated route at Catford and at Stagecoach Selkent as a whole, but that was a year off yet.

When sighted on a diversion of the 185 through Victoria bus station on 16 January 2000, Catford's **T 810** (OHV 810Y) was still carrying the original format of Stagecoach Selkent identification, with fleetname above the radiator grille and fleetnumber alongside. Although starting at Catford, this bus had spent from April 1990 to November 1998 at Bromley before returning, and would come off service in April 2001.

T 828 (A828 SUL) was another Catford lifer, or so it still appeared when it was sighted at Lewisham on 23 June 2000. As it turned out, after Catford had no further need of it, it was transferred to Barking in March 2001 and spent the last three months of its life there.

Stagecoach's practice nationally was to put its buses' fleetnumbers twice on front and back, at each corner, but that didn't sit well in London as it meant there was nothing on the side, i.e. if you missed identifying the bus from the front, you wouldn't get it at all. **T 812** (OHV 812Y), which spent all its life at Catford between July 1983 and March 2001, demonstrates at Canada Water as night falls on 13 December 2000.

Another to carry the original Stagecoach Selkent format of fleetnumber and fleetname positioning into the 21st century, T 815 (OHV 815Y) was also a Catford lifer and on 22 April 2000 is seen at the southern end of Lewisham High Street. Only one of its opening windows at the front upper deck has been replaced, producing a 'one-eyed' appearance. After the 185 was lost, this bus continued on until the 136 was converted to TA operation in February 2001.

Accordingly, T 815 (OHV 815Y) kept the rear-facing results of its September 1996 repaint, which included a reflective numberplate with 'Stagecoach' at the base. On 7 July 2000 it is seen queuing at the top of Tooley Street for the right turn into London Bridge.

Speaking of repaints, the very last to affect the Stagecoach Titans were effected ever so slightly incorrectly in that the usual black of the radiator was applied over the moulding of the grille, where it didn't customarily go. That made the grilles look uncomfortably bloated, as on **T 680** (OHV 680Y) at Lewisham on 22 April 2000. Having come from Bromley in February 1999, this bus would last at Catford until December 2000.

T 836 (A836 SUL) was another repaint where the black went over the edges of the radiator grille. The repaint itself was much appreciated, however, as they always are, and Stagecoach's reputation for looking after their vehicles was generally good. Beginning and ending at Catford, this bus had spent the middle part of its career at Bromley, with a short spell at Plumstead, and on 18 July 2000 it is seen in Tooley Street at the Tower Bridge end. It was withdrawn in March 2001.

On 16 October 2000 Catford's **T 740** (OHV 740Y) pauses at London Bridge with the tallest City of London tower of the time in the background. Having served in order at Bexleyheath, Sidcup, Ash Grove, Bromley, Bexleyheath (again) and Bromley (again), it came to Catford in November 1998 and lasted until September 2001 as one of its last garage's small band of holdouts.

Other than a year spent at Bromley, **T 829** (A829 SUL) counted itself a lifetime Catford motor, and on 7 July 2000 was in Tooley Street on the 47. It would be withdrawn at the end of the year.

On 11 May 2000 **T 841** (A841 SUL) is about to climb Bromley High Street towards Bromley South station. Based at the garage since December 1995, it would come off in October 2000.

T 842 (A842 SUL) spent nine years at Catford, three years at Plumstead and five at Bromley, where it finished its London career in February 2001. On 22 April 2000 it is setting off from Bexleyheath on a route that was meant to be SLD-operated (Dart SLFs) but frequently saw Titans and VAs.

On 22 August 2000 Catford's **T 868** (A868 SUL) has set off from Shoreditch and is heading south with an Enfield M of Arriva London North in hot pursuit. Its third separate spell at Catford was in its tenth year at this point, but would come to an end in February 2001.

Wearing its squashed-number blinds with pride, Catford's **T 545** (KYV 545X) is at Lewisham on 12 January 2001. In the six weeks to come it would spend time on loan to London Easylink on the 185 and then submit to withdrawal.

T 842 (A842 SUL) is seen on 14 October 2000 in the part of Bromley served by buses ever since the northern end of the High Street was pedestrianised. It had four more months to go at Bromley.

Although three of the Leyland-engined Titans were sold as soon as withdrawals commenced at the end of 1992, LBL got their money's worth by converting the rest to Gardner power, and six remained in service until the start of 2001. **T 882** (A882 SUL) was one such, based at Catford again (where it had started) since November 1997 and seen on 29 September 2000 at London Bridge.

2000 was to be the last full year in service for **T 882** (A882 SUL); seen in Lewisham High Street on 2 December of that year, it would come off in March 2001.

Transferred from North Street to Catford in July 1998, **T 536** (KYV 536X) is seen heeling round the roundabout at the bottom of the bus-only section of Lewisham High Street on 12 January 2001. It was withdrawn in March but reactivated to become one of half a dozen holdouts that would keep the Titan alive at Catford, and at Stagecoach Selkent as a whole, until the autumn. Not to be the very last, however, it finally came off in September.

The contribution to the Titan story of Catford and Bromley garages came to a close in 2001, but before that, in shimmering winter sunshine on 23 January 2000 at Lewisham bus station, we see **T 883** (A883 SUL) from the former and **T 961** (A961 SYE) from the latter. Both have managed to keep hold of their opening front upper-deck windows, though the foglights on each are long gone and replaced by flush bumpers. Formerly Leyland L11-engined, T 883 was withdrawn in March 2001, T 961 leaving before that, in October 2000.

On 20 January 2001, the day this photo at London Bridge was taken, Stagecoach Selkent's Catford garage lost the 185, but could still supply Titans enough for pairs like **T 749** (OHV 749Y) and **T 880** (A880 SUL) to find themselves in evidence on the 47. Transferred to Catford in October 1998 after a decade at garages across the river, T 749 was withdrawn in March 2001, while T 880, its life prolonged through the replacement of its Leyland TL11 engine with a Gardner unit, came off in the same month.

The famous 'Rickys' were seven Titans registered with RYK-Y plates when deliveries outpaced the OHV-Y registrations booked for them in July 1983 and it wasn't considered expedient to wait until the new A-registrations were legal to carry on the road. **T 816** (RYK 816Y) was the first, and spent all its life at Catford. Seen in Lewisham High Street on 17 February 2001, it would be withdrawn in March. Fittingly, a 'Ricky', T 822, was one of the last two Titans in service at Catford on 5 October.

Massive withdrawals of Titans in February and March 2001 removed the type from Bromley and left only seven in service at Catford by the spring. The highest-numbered of them was **T 848** (A848 SUL), based at Catford for the vast majority of its life but now reduced to helping out on the 47 and 160 pending delivery of further new Tridents. On 6 July it is seen at Eltham, with three months left to go.

The oldest of the seven Catford holdouts was **T 456** (KYV 456X), which had spent its first ten years at West Ham and seven thereafter at Bow before coming to Catford in March 1999. By 2001 special trips had to be made to hunt down these surviving Titans, and 10 September of that year at Rushey Green has proven a success.

By the end of September 2001 just Ts 456 and 822 were left at Catford, and a chance shot as the sun sets over Forest Hill on 29 September caught **T 456** (KYV 456X) away from the 47 one last time. Both buses were withdrawn after service on Friday 5 October, both of them on the 47, and that was the end of the Titan at Stagecoach Selkent.

BLUE TRIANGLE

T 349 (KYV 349X) only served from two garages; Walthamstow since delivery at the end of 1981, and after that closed on 23 November 1991, Brixton. It was converted to a trainer in March 1993 and remained that way across privatisation until sale to Ensign in August 1995. Blue Triangle made it one of their first Titan acquisitions and painted it in this most elegant livery. It would thus find its way back onto revenue-earning London service when the 60 was partially allocated to Blue Triangle on 29 August 1998, on which day it is seen in central Croydon. It was damaged in the container fall at Rainham on 27 October 2002 and sold not long after that.

When the 60's intended permanent contractor Driver Express defaulted spectacularly, Blue Triangle's role was increased and it ended up in overall supervision of the route, wrangling an unlikely collection of operators to keep the service going on an emergency timetable until the next winner along, Capital Logistics, prepared itself to take over. Former London Central Titans were gathered, and T 898 (A898 SYE), seen in Croydon on 27 February 1999, had already spent a temporary spell with Capital Citybus, filling in on the 1 until its own Metrobuses could be readied.

Another ex-New Cross T drafted by Blue Triangle for the 60's crazy winter was **T 908** (A908 SYE), seen heading north from West Croydon on 6 February 1999.

Unlike T 898, **T 908** (A908 SYE) was kept in the long term and received a repaint into Blue Triangle's 1999 livery with more red and less cream. It is seen at Brooklands runway on 9 April 2000, during the occasion of that year's Cobham bus rally.

T 1095 (B95 WUV) spent fifteen and a half years in south-east London, serving at Plumstead, Bromley, New Cross (with which it became a London Central bus) and finally Bexleyheath. However, after its sale it found itself back on Plumstead's main route when a few extras were added by Blue Triangle. On 9 July 2002 it is seen coming up to the Elephant, where these short-workings terminated.

When the 185's operator, London Easylink, was compelled to come off the road on 21 August 2002, Blue Triangle's buses abandoned their supporting role on the 53 and rode to the rescue. On the afternoon of 24 August **T 33** (WYV 33T) is seen in Lewisham High Street, with only rudimentary blinds so far. Blue Triangle amassed Ts from the very beginning and very end of the fleetnumber run, and this one was acquired from Stagecoach East London after an epic 22-year career at Hornchurch and then North Street (with two brief flirtations with Walthamstow before and after overhaul).

At the Victoria end of the 185 on the evening of 23 August 2002, we see **Ts 1101** (B101 WUV) and **1095** (B95 WUV). Differences between badges, numberplates and bumpers are evident, but the company livery had settled on this attractive take on classic red. T 1101's 'London Transport' career had been worked out of Bromley, Catford and then Bromley again. It lasted until 2008 at Blue Triangle and was then bought for preservation, joining T 1030 in its age group.

When Blue Triangle won the 248, its intended East Lancs-bodied Dennis Tridents were slow arriving, so the company resorted to the tried and trusted Titan, taking several just coming out of service from North Street of Stagecoach East London. There wasn't enough time to repaint them fully, so just the cream livery embellishments were applied, as on **T 9** (WYV 9T) in Romford on 13 October 2001.

T 4 (WYV 4T) was another ex-North Street veteran acquired by Blue Triangle to bed in the 248, but unlike T 9, remained in all-over red. On 23 June 2002 it is seen on a District Line replacement service coming through South Kensington.

On the same rail job and at the same location as T 4 is **T 11** (WYV 11T), acquired in August 2001. This bus lasted until 2009, eventually donating its parts.

T 2 (THX 402S) was a special case as it wound down with Stagecoach East London and remained so upon its sale to Blue Triangle in August 2001. Restored to full original condition including an authentic set of early indicators and sidelights, it became the company's flagship for the second-generation OPO double-deck era. One particularly auspicious role for it was when it turned out on 4 June 2004, the 8's gala last day as a Routemaster route; it is seen in Bow garage's doorway.

SOVEREIGN

Borehamwood Travel Services, better known under its BTS abbreviation, were the first London operator to take second-hand Titans as they poured out of service at the end of 1992. The five subsequent acquisitions made a nice complement to the Northern Counties-bodied Leyland Olympian fleet already operated on the 114. Later in the decade, the Sovereign fleetname was adopted and the Titans became known under numeric fleetnumbers in the seven hundreds. **706** (OHV 706Y), therefore, seen at Harrow bus station on 28 July 2000, had been T 706 in its LBL days.

Under the same renumbering programme at Sovereign, T 620 became **720** (NUW 620Y) and was also converted to single-door configuration for its assistance on the 114, 292 and later on still, the 13. On 6 July 2000 it is seen approaching Harrow bus station from the other direction. Titans operated from Sovereign until August 2001.

METROLINE CS

After the acquisition of Atlas Bus and the conversion of its route 52 to M operation, Metroline kept the best of the Titans and put them to use with its Contract Services offshoot. On 31 May 1998 **T 432** (KYV 432X) is seen at Alexandra Palace station on a rail replacement service. It lasted until August 1999 here, after which it was sold.

T 375 (KYV 375X) was another Metroline Contract Services Titan, and in this 7 June 1999 shot captured from a double-decker departing Brent Cross, was displaying blinds for Hertfordshire school contract 832B. It too was withdrawn and sold in August 1999.

FIRST CAPITAL

On 14 November 1998 the 1 was transferred from London Central to First Capital, which was accumulating Metrobuses from its CentreWest partner. Until they were all acquired and repainted, First Capital hired twelve of the route's previous complement of Titans, one of which was **T 894** (A894 SYE), seen in Tower Bridge Road on 4 January 1999. After its loan to Dagenham, T 894 came back to London Central but this time was allocated to Bexleyheath and spent until April 2000 there.

T 898 (A898 SYE) was also caught in Tower Bridge Road on 4 January 1999, and its overall state can be compared with that of its former and current sibling, in terms of numberplates, windows and lights. This bus was sold after its spell at First Capital, landing at Blue Triangle, which fruther loaned it to Capital Logistics for that company's troubled first few weeks on the 60.

The cautionary tale of Durham Travel Services' London Easylink operation would fill a book by itself, perhaps one with a plain brown cover if the allegations therein have any truth to them, but for the purposes of this particular publication, all that needs explained is the company's use of Titans in the first few weeks of the 185's operation. Between 20 January and 12 February 2001, eleven Titans were hired from Stagecoach Selkent, all of which were from the same Catford stock that had worked on the 185 prior to the change of operators.

On 20 January 2001 **T 546** (KYV 546X) is seen at Lewisham bus station, where **T 771** (OHV 771Y) is also laying over when photographed on 10 February. The 185's first fortnight with London Easylink was to prove the last hurrah for both of these Titans, which were sold to Ensign in March.

SULLIVAN BUSES

Having begun in 1997 with just T 85, Sullivan Buses took to the Titan with enthusiasm and built its rail-replacement business upon them. A later acquisition, and one much loved, was **T 747** (OHV 747Y), which had been the former Golden Jubilee Titan and now resumed that marvellous livery with a flourish. Seen on display at Barking's annual RT rally on 31 March 2002, it was not to last much longer, being damaged in an accident, but repairs were eventually undertaken and it survives today.

Acquired in March 2002 from White Rose, **T 1074** (A74 THX) had spent most of the latter half of its London career as a Camberwell bus latterly out of London Central. On 9 March 2002 it is performing rail replacement duties at Alexandra Palace station.

T 995 (A995 SYE) came to Sullivan Buses in June 2001, having finished its London career at New Cross of London Central. The latter portion of 2003 was famous for the massive number of ageing second-hand Titans and Metrobuses pressed into service from all ends of the capital when the Northern Line fell apart on multiple occasions. When the buses were out of service, they could be espied laying over in the car park behind East Finchley station, where not just this Titan, but M 563 and Blue Triangle's inimitable RT 3871, could be seen on 30 October 2003.

Sullivan Buses bought **T 889** (A889 SYE) from London Central in April 2000; it had recently come out of service when PVLs replaced it at Bexleyheath. This one had a red bumper and black numberplate for a unique look within its pack of Titans, and on 16 May 2004 could be seen at Leytonstone covering for the Central Line.

By the time **T 1098** (B98 WUV) was prepared for service following its acqusition from London Central in June 2001, the numberplate characters had been forced to shrink in width by seven millimetres, producing a not particularly attractive result. Also caught at Leytonstone on 16 May 2004, it was sporting a website address, a new accoutrement for the modern age.

WHITE ROSE

Like Sullivan Buses, White Rose Travel brought back classic London Transport liveries for their acquired Metrobuses and Titans helping out the Underground in its time of need. **T 794** (OHV 794Y) was nothing short of spectacular, recreating the *Aldenham Diplomat* livery best known on T 66 in 1983. This bus had spent its first two years alongside Ms on the 18 before settling at New Cross, where it finished at the end of 1997. On 9 May 1999 it is seen at Liverpool Street station.

T 756 (OHV 756Y) received a more conventional London Transport livery when it was acquired in February 2000 after a London career that both began and ended at Bexleyheath. On 14 May 2000 it was taking passengers from Wokingham station to the Crowthorne test centre, where a bus rally was being held.

IMPERIAL

Imperial of Rainham accumulated a total of five Titans, and painted all of them into this splendid green livery with classic gold leaf fleetnames. **T 302** (KYV 302X), taken in August 1999 after last working from Metroline Contract Services, is seen at the 2001 incarnation of Cobham bus rally.

At North Weald on 24 June 2001 we see Imperial's **T 379** (KYV 379X), the London career of which had finished at Stagecoach East London's North Street garage. It spent seven years with Imperial.

Z&S

A particular favourite of the author's, **T 818** (RYK 818Y) was the first Titan he ever travelled on. It spent its entire London career at Catford and was acquired by Aylesbury-based Z&S in April 2001. Still in the faded red livery in which it left Stagecoach Selkent, it is doing rail replacement work at Swiss Cottage on 26 July 2003.

T 963 (A963 SYE) was the joint last Titan at Peckham, the penultimate London Central garage to operate the type. When it passed to Z&S in April 2003, it received a lower-deck repaint incorporating a blue skirt, and it is in that livery that it is seen covering the Metropolitan Line at Wembley Park early in the morning of 9 August 2003.

WEST KENT

West Kent Buses, otherwise a second-hand bus dealership, entered the rail-replacement fray in 2003 with two superb liveries. **T 1124** (B124 WUV) came in December 2002 after a spell at Stagecoach East Kent, and is seen on 9 August 2003 at Wembley Park.

West Kent's second livery, adorning **T 442** (KYV 442X) at Wembley Park on 9 August 2003, was rather simpler. This bus had also spent the second half of the 1990s with a provincial Stagecoach firm, in this case Sussex Coastline, but before that had last worked from Bromley in October 1995.

The livery chosen for Legg's Travel **T 523** (KYV 523X) was unorthdox, but it also had T 79 with an equally random combination of colours. After an extremely varied career in London by comparison with fellow Titans in its delivery range, T 523 had passed to Stagecoach South Coast Buses in 1995 and it was from here that Mike Nash picked it up for resale to Legg's. It was operating the shuttle service between Cobham Bus Museum and Brooklands runway on 7 April 2002, and is seen at the latter.

Mullany's Starline of Watford had two Titans and **T 896** (A896 SYE) was one of them, acquired from Westlink in September 1996 and lasting ten further years. It is working the shuttle service during 2000's incarnation of Cobham bus rally.

The state of the Northern Line in 2003 invited anyone who could put a bus into action to come and help out on replacing it at weekends, and one more such Titan operator was Shamrock Travel of Abercynon in south Wales. **T 973** (A973 SYE) had come out of service at Peckham in February 2000, but when photographed at the bus park behind East Finchley station on 30 October 2003, was still in as-acquired condition.

TOURS

The furious competition seen on the London tour services when the concept was deregulated in the early 1980s gave way to a small number of companies of a size that could sustain themselves against one another. Affiliated on and off with Ensign, London Pride fielded the obligatory Metrobuses and Titans, converting them to open-top configuration. **282** (WYV 67T) was born T 67 and had already spent a second London career as London & Country/ Londonlinks 925 before coming to London Pride in January 1997. On 22 May 1998 it is seen at Cambridge Circus.

353 (CUL 78V) was also an ex-Londonlinks Titan, known there as 913 and in this case retaining its exit door. The accent to the red base livery is gold on this bus, seen near Piccadilly Circus on 25 August 1998.

281 (WYV 43T) completes the trio of London Pride Titans acquired when Londonlinks replaced them, though in this case T 43 was briefly with AML Coaches before its move to London & Country as 927. On 3 September 1999 it is seen at Tottenham Court Road.

LBL's old Leaside District came to the Titan rather by accident, when the surplus developing in east London had to be redeployed, and once those buses had reached their own sell-by date, some of them were repurposed as trainers. A little later still, a handful of Ts were refitted as tour buses and in that way were handed down to the Leaside Travel commercial concern developed prior to privatisation. That particular process took the whole operation to Cowie, whose two diagonal stripes were incorporated into a new livery seen on **T 83** (CUL 83V) at Trafalgar Square on 2 August 1999. Later still, these open-toppers received a variant of Arriva livery and lasted until mid-2001.

Leaside Travel's original livery derived from LBL's tapegrey, with gold accents added. **T 69** (UJN 335V) was twice re-registered, spending its first fourteen years under CUL 69V and then assuming 70 CLT in January 1994 before this unused mark was allocated in February 1998. On 26 September 1999 it is seen at Showbus at Duxford.

Few Titan liveries were as splendid as that of Big Bus, a later addition to the pack of open-top tour firms but soon to become highly successful. The company took a strong liking to the Titan and operated large numbers of them for close to a decade. **T 1024** (A624 THV) was acquired in 1998 after leaving Peckham (London Central) and is seen on 9 May 1999 turning from London Bridge into Tooley Street.

The only trouble with operating open-top buses in London is the strong likelihood that the weather will fail on you whenever it pleases, so Big Bus warded off this eventuality by devising a PVC roof that could be rolled on and off. **T 781** (OHV 781Y), last of London Central's Camberwell garage, demonstrates at Bank on 20 August 1999.

The Big Bus Company had its own fleetnumbering system, which unfortunately was so complicated that it's best explained elsewhere, especially since the fleetnumbers were, for the most part, minuscule. This one, however, calls itself **LB 4712** (OHV 712Y) and was once T 712. It is seen at Hyde Park Corner on 2 October 2003.

PRESERVED

It was wondered at the time why the marvellous livery on **T 172** (CUL 172V) was not seen fit to continue after the Queen's Jubilee Year 2002, not to mention why such an elderly Titan was repainted into London Central's livery of the time with mere months envisaged remaining, but the result stood a better chance of preservation for it, and so it was to prove. When seen at North Weald on 29 June 2003 it was under the ownership of LR Travel, and even after that was acquired by Sullivan Buses for a last few years on rail-replacement work.

T 369 (KYV 369X) had by 1994 aged past a suitable cut-off for service, it was felt by New Cross, its final garage at the time, so it was converted to a trainer and spent three more years as such, spanning the privatisation of its home under London Central. In December 1997 it was sold to Skylark Travel and turned out with this smart wraparound ad for a company that could be relied upon for the parts and mechanical needs of not only preservationists, but existing companies nearby. On 28 June 1998 it is displayed at that particular year's incarnation of North Weald bus rally.

As the Titan neared its end in service at the turn of the century, one last role remained to selected representatives, and that was as in-house preservation pieces. **T 1** (THX 401S) had, to be fair, occupied this role ever since its first repaint back into the livery it had carried when new, as far back as 1983, and Stagecoach East London continued the tradition, keeping it in service right to the end at North Street. After that it popped up on specials, in this instance the gala retirement of Routemasters from the 8 in the three weeks up to 4 June 2004. When seen at Holborn on 16 May, it was being assisted on this task by Metrobus M 1 out of Metroline.

On 2 April 2006 at Wisley airfield **T 961** (A961 SYE) looks splendid as it recalls its original posting at Walworth, which lasted until the garage's first closure on 2 November 1985. It was later treated to a charming 'what if' livery that imagined what might have happened if the classic Green Line livery had reached the Titan.

One of the best-known Titans in preservation today is **T 1030** (A630 THV), for most of its 17-year career a Bromley bus and in this 16 September 2007 picture at Duxford remembering one of that garage's shorter-lived routes.

At the other end of the preservation age spectrum is **T 6** (WYV 6T), looking absolutely perfect with every feature correct, particularly the numberplate transfers, which don't have a commercially-available equivalent font and have to be made up specially by a firm in Essex. In 2007 Cobham bus rally had to be held at Longcross test track, and the event (in stark contrast to what happened the year after!) was blessed with perfect weather.

The London bus preservation field often finds itself called upon to represent itself in other parts of the country, especially when those parts take former London models to their own hearts. The Titan served a distinguished decade in Liverpool when acquired in large numbers by Merseybus, and under the banners of MTL, Arriva, GTL and finally Stagecoach, merited their own gala Last Day. This took place on 4 February 2006 with a procession to and from the Wirral of Ts 337, 624 and 850 from the outgoing Gillmoss operation, backed up by T 1 from Stagecoach East London and this one, **T 910** (A910 SYE) in preservation locally. During that afternoon it is seen opposite the Liver Building.

BIBLIOGRAPHY

Books
The London Bus Review of ... (1973-1992), LOTS 1974-1994
The London Titan, Matthew Wharmby, Ian Allan 2008

Magazines, Supplements, Articles and Periodicals
The London Bus (TLB), LOTS, monthly
London Bus Magazine (LBM), LOTS, quarterly
TLB Extra, LOTS, yearly
BUSES magazine, Ian Allan, monthly
SUP-44A London Bus Disposals – Where are they Now? March 2008, LOTS 2008.

Websites and Groups
Ian's Bus Stop (www.countrybus.org)
London Bus Routes by Ian Armstrong (www.londonbuses.co.uk)

Barking's **T 578** (NUW 578Y) is seen in Barking town centre on 14 June 1998. It had arrived here in August 1992, having previously served at Plumstead, Sidcup, Plumstead again and Chalk Farm. Privatisation fixed it in place with Stagecoach East London and it would be withdrawn from Barking in July 2001.